THE WORLD OF SCIENCE

BIRDS

THE WORLD OF SCIENCE
BIRDS

MAURICE BURTON

Facts On File Publications
New York, New York ● Bicester, England

BIRDS

First published in the United States of America in
1985 by Facts on File, Inc., 460 Park Avenue South,
New York, N.Y.10016

First published in Great Britain in 1985 by Orbis
Publishing Limited, London

**Library of Congress Cataloging in Publication
Data**

Main entry under title:

World of Science

   Includes index.
   Summary: A twenty-five volume encyclopedia of
scientific subjects, designed for eight- to twelve-year-
olds. One volume is entirely devoted to projects.
   1. Science—Dictionaries, Juvenile.   1. Science—
Dictionaries
Q121.J86   1984   500   84-1654

ISBN: 0-8160-1063-3

Printed in Yugoslavia
10 9 8 7 6 5 4 3 2

Consultant editors
Eleanor Felder, former managing editor, *New Book of
Knowledge*
James Neujahr, Dean of the School of Education, City
College of New York
Ethan Signer, Professor of Biology, Massachusetts
Institute of Technology
J. Tuzo Wilson, Director General, Ontario Science
Centre

Previous pages A
flock of lesser
flamingoes at dawn,
beside Lake Nakuru,
Kenya, East Africa.

Editor Penny Clarke
Designer Roger Kohn

CONTENTS

Note: There are some unusual words in this book. They are explained in the Glossary on page 62. The first time each word is used in the text it is printed in *italics*.

▲ A superb close-up photograph of the head of a young crowned crane, showing details of the feathers.

WHAT IS A BIRD?

BIRDS ARE . . .

If an animal can fly, has a beak, lays eggs, and is covered with feathers we know immediately that it is a bird. In fact, it is so unlike any other living thing that most people speak of birds and animals, as if birds did not belong to the animal kingdom. So it really is very easy to say what a bird is. Or is it?

If you think about it for a moment, you will realize that birds are not the only animals that fly. There are bats and there are also many insects that fly. There are also flying fishes, too. You may also read of such things as flying squirrels, flying lizards and flying frogs, but these merely glide. They take off from trees, stretching out folds of skin on their bodies to act as parachutes to keep them airborne for a short while before they land on another tree.

The flight of bats, insects and birds is different. They use powered flight, beating their wings to keep themselves up in the air. Using powered flight they can also take off from the ground, twist and turn in the air and fly very long distances without stopping. So birds are not the only creatures that fly.

Then again, birds are not the only animals with beaks. There are, for example, those animals that are called beaked whales. So birds are not the only creatures with beaks.

Birds are not the only animals to lay eggs. Many *reptiles* produce eggs with leathery shells. So that is no help in deciding whether a creature is a bird or not.

Feathers
That leaves feathers. In fact feathers are the one thing all birds have and all other animals do not have. A bird's feathers protect it from the weather. They insulate a bird from the heat of the sun. They also keep out the cold. And they protect it from getting too wet. They also play a very important part in forming the wings used in flying. The tail feathers are used as a balancer while the bird is in the air, for steering while the bird is flying and as a brake when the bird is slowing down when it needs to land.

The way feathers are made is quite remarkable. Each feather is made up of a shaft or *quill* and a *vane*. The vane is the flat part. There is also a small tuft of down near the base of the vane known as the *aftershaft*.

The vane is made up of numerous hair-like filaments on either side of the shaft. These are known as barbs. Each barb has a row of smaller filaments on each side. These are called barbules and are hooked at their tips. The way these work is rather similar to a zip-fastener. If the vane becomes crumpled or disarranged you can pass it between your finger and thumb and the vane then looks as good as new. A bird does the same by running the feathers, one at a time, through its beak.

▲ Parrots have a powerful hooked beak for cracking and peeling hard nuts. This is the beak of a macaw, one of the parrot family.

▲ A duck's bill is wide and flat. It is used to scoop up mud. The water is strained off and any small animals and plants that are left behind are swallowed.

▲ The sparrow's conical beak is used for cracking and de-husking seeds.

▲ The woodpecker uses its chisel-like beak to drill holes in wood in the search for insects.

▲ The sharp hook-like beak of an eagle is for tearing the flesh of its prey.

▲ The pelican uses the large bag under its beak as a scoop-net for fishing.

◄ The skeleton of a bird with the main flight feathers of one wing left in position. Compare the size of the wing bones with those of the legs.

Preening

When a bird runs its feathers through its beak it is said to be preening. This means it is tidying any feathers that have become untidy. All birds spend much of their time preening, especially after they have been bathing or dust-bathing.

While preening they also oil their feathers. They get the oil by pressing the beak on an oil-gland near the base of the tail. Then, as they pass each feather through the beak it is not only tidied but is oiled at the same time, to help keep out the wet.

▲ A male pintail preening himself. Although all birds preen themselves, it is particularly important for water birds. As they preen they oil their feathers, so ensuring that they remain waterproof.

THE FIRST BIRDS

► Fossilized remains of *Archaeopteryx*, the ancestor of today's birds. The wing feathers have left clear impressions in the rocks.

About 140 million years ago there lived in Europe an animal that looked like a bird but had the bones of a lizard. Its body was covered with feathers and it had a kind of beak, but this beak had teeth like the teeth of a lizard. Instead of stubby tail with a fan of feathers, like most birds today, it had a long tail, like a lizard, with pairs of feathers along its length. In short, this animal was half-bird, half-reptile. Scientists called it *Archaeopteryx,* which means ancient-wing.

▼ Adélie penguins queuing up to jump off an ice floe into the cold waters of the Antarctic Ocean.

Only a very few specimens of this fossil have been found, in a special sandstone in Bavaria, in West Germany. It was a lucky accident that these few fossils were preserved, even luckier that they were found. As it is, they show us that the first birds were lizards that grew feathers instead of scales. They also show that Archaeopteryx did not fly, in the true sense. Instead it probably climbed into trees, jumped into the air and then glided to the ground.

As time went by some of its descendants lost even the power to glide and just walked or ran. They became the running birds. By far the largest number started to beat their wings as they glided and so learned to fly. Their descendants became what we now speak of as the flying birds, although as time passed even some of these have become flightless or use the wings so little that they seem almost to be flightless.

THE POWER OF FLIGHT

There is a great difference between a lizard that can glide and an animal that can fly hundreds or thousands of miles non-stop. The most important change the first flying birds had to make was to develop lighter bodies. They did this mainly in two ways. First, they developed hollow bones. Secondly, they grew air-filled bags inside their bodies. These are called air-sacs and they lie between the other organs in the body such as the heart, lungs, and stomach. The air-sacs are connected to the lungs, which is how they get their air.

The next thing they had to do was to grow extra strong muscles to beat the wings. In fact as much as a fifth of a bird's weight may be in these flight-muscles, which form what we call the breast when we eat chicken or turkey.

Muscles cannot work unless they are fastened to something solid at each end. The large muscles that form the breast of a bird are fastened at one end on the *breastbone*, at the other to the bones of the wings.

Because the flight-muscles are large they need a large surface to which they can be fastened. So the breastbone is large and, in addition, it has a crest or keel, to increase this surface.

Flying demands more energy than any other form of locomotion. All the internal workings of a bird are speeded up to supply this energy quickly. In small birds, such as sparrows and robins, the breathing rate is 250 times a minute.

In contrast we take 12 breaths (in and out) every minute. Our heart beat is 70 a minute but in sparrows and robins it may be as much as 500 a minute.

There is another difference. A bird's lungs are small. They take up only 2% of the bird's body against the 5% our lungs take up. But birds can manage with such small lungs because their breathing is extremely efficient. When a bird breathes in, air not only fills the lungs but passes into the air-sacs connected to them. As it breaths out, the lungs are emptied and air is then drawn in from the air-sacs into the lungs, giving it a second quantity of oxygen.

◄ Swifts spend most of their lives on the wing – wheeling and gliding as they search for food.

▲ An Indian white-backed vulture swoops to the ground, spreading out its powerful wings to act as a brake.

◄ Hummingbirds can hover in flight. To do this they move their wings in a figure-of-eight movement, not up and down.

THE SENSE-ORGANS

▲ The position of the eyes in the little bittern (**above**) and the short-eared owl (**right**) are in marked contrast. The owl actually has a very limited field of vision, but to make up for this it can turn its head to look over its shoulder, as in the picture, very easily and quickly.

Sight

Birds need sharp eyesight, particularly high-flying birds such as eagles and hawks, which must be able to see their prey on the ground. Birds also have good hearing, but they do not have much use for a sense of smell. Birds that hunt insects in the air or on plants usually have eyes on the sides of the head. The left eye scans the area to the left, the right eye does the same for the right, so such birds can see almost all around without having to turn their heads. They can, in fact, look at two things at once, one on the left side and one on the right. If they want to look closely at something they can turn both eyes forwards and look 'cross-eyed' at it.

Birds-of-prey, such as hawks and owls, have eyes that look straight forward. So a hawk or falcon looking for small animals on the ground can focus on small objects a great distance away.

Colour vision in birds

Most animals do not see colours. That is they are colour-blind. They see the world mainly in shades of black and white, as we see a picture on a non-colour television screen. Scientists once thought that some animals, such as dogs, cats and horses, were colour-blind. But research has shown that they can see a few colours. Certain insects have good colour vision. Bees are a good example. But they do not always see colours as we see them.

Birds see colours much as we do, but they can also see ultra-violet which is invisible to us. It is hardly surprising that birds can see colours. The brilliance of their feathers and the way they use patches of colour in their courtship displays suggest good colour vision. Tests have been carried out with budgerigars, parrots, canaries, farmyard poultry, pigeons, kestrels and thrushes.

One interesting experiment was carried out with a tame rook, a European member of the crow family. Beads of the same size and shape, but different colours, were scattered on the floor of its aviary. The rook collected the beads and hid them under the turf. It first collected all the red beads. Then it collected the white beads, followed by the brown, blue and yellow.

The rook did this many times, dealing with each colour in turn. Although it did not always collect the colours in the same order, it never mixed beads of different colours.

Hearing

Although some owls, the 'eared owls', have what look like ears, these are only tufts of feathers. Unlike *mammals* no bird has external ear-flaps for collecting sound waves and directing them onto the ear-drum. In fact the openings to a bird's ears are covered by its head-feathers. Even so, all birds have acute hearing, and owls can pounce on mice just by listening to their movements on the ground.

It is difficult to know how far birds use their sense of smell. Kiwis find earthworms by smell and some seabirds seem to use it to find their food. But although scientists have done much research on this topic, we still know very little about birds' sense of smell and how they use it.

We do not know much more about birds' sense of taste, although they must use it to choose the right foods. However, we do know that parrots have a good sense of taste.

▼ The kiwi moves like a ghost through the undergrowth at night, the only bird that depends almost entirely on its sense of smell for its food.

FEEDING AND DIGESTION

Birds have no lips or teeth. Their bony jaws, called *mandibles*, are covered with horn forming a beak or bill, used for grasping and breaking up food. Beaks vary greatly in size and shape, according to the type of food the bird eats.

Because flying demands so much energy a bird needs plenty of food. This means it must have an efficient digestive system.

When swallowed the food enters a narrow tube called the gullet. In many birds, especially seed-eaters, the lower part of the gullet swells out to form a *crop* where food is stored before it passes into the stomach.

The stomach is divided into two parts. The first part has the digestive juices. The second part, called the *gizzard*, has very strong muscular walls. In it, food is ground down. Many birds swallow small stones and grit which end up in the gizzard where they help in the grinding process.

The digested food passes into the intestine where it is taken into the blood stream and carried to all parts of the body.

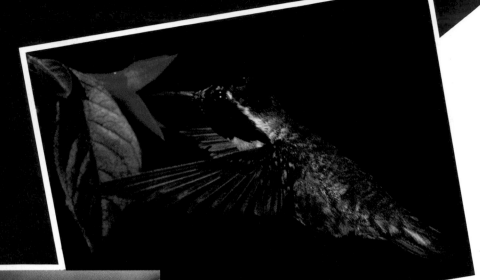

▲ A male Costa's hummingbird hovers in front of a flower as it collects the nectar on which it feeds.

◄ The red-billed oxpecker lives in Africa and feeds principally on the parasites that infect wild and domestic cattle, as this one is doing.

▲ A goosander photographed underwater as it catches a fish. Notice its very streamlined shape as it swims.

◄ An African tawny eagle crouches over its kill – a smaller bird.

SONGS AND SINGING

Birds are well-known for their voices. Most make only short calls, but some have longer songs made up of musical sounds. Many also mimic other sounds, even imitating human speech.

Calls form a kind of language, used by members of a flock to keep in touch or to tell each other of danger. Calls are also used between male and female or parents and young. Song is part of this language. When a male bird has chosen a territory it advertises this by singing from several different 'singing posts' within that territory. He will also sing vigorously if a rival male enters his territory. Used in this way song is a threat, warning the other bird to go away or it will be attacked.

On the other hand, the male bird's song attracts females when they are looking for a mate. When the male and a female have paired, his singing continues as a means of warning away intruders, so protecting not only the territory but also the nest, the hen and her eggs or young.

So it follows that, with few exceptions, it is the male which sings most. It also follows that he sings most during the breeding season. In some species of birds the females sing, too. For example female European robins have their own territories in winter and sing to defend them. Recent research suggests that birds may sing for their own enjoyment as well as for advertising a territory, attracting a mate or for threatening a rival. This is, that they sing as we do, for enjoyment.

▲ This little mistletoe flowerpecker is incubating her eggs in the nest she has built of grasses and spiders' webs. These birds live in Australia, although other types of flowerpecker live in India and south-east Asia.

NEST-BUILDING

Most birds make a nest into which to lay their eggs. The nests provide protection for the eggs and help keep them warm. Some cuckoos and most cowbirds lay their eggs in the nests of other birds (page 40). A few birds take over old, deserted nests. There are also a very few kinds of bird that make no nest at all. The guillemot, for example, lays its eggs on the bare rocks of cliff ledges. The females of the emperor and king penguins lay a single egg and hold it on their feet.

Nests vary from one kind of bird to another. They may be no more than saucer-shaped scrapes in the ground with a few pieces of dried grass for the lining. Or they may be a massive tower of sticks with some soft material on top for the eggs to lie on. Such large nests mean a great deal of work, as do some of the smaller nests. The longtailed tit, with a body only a few centimetres long, builds an oval nest of moss, spiders' webs and lichen. The nest is finished with a lining of feathers. There may be as many as 2,000 in one nest – a tremendous amount of work for a tiny bird.

Although most nests are simple and cup-shaped, there are many variations to this pattern. The tailor bird, of tropical Africa and Asia, sews together the edges of a large leaf with strands of grass. Then it builds a nest inside the folded leaf.

Usually it is the female that builds the nest but in many species the male helps. In some species, for example wrens, the male does all the building leaving the female to line the nest.

Some birds will decorate their nests with flowers. The common starling is one. The decoration seems to have no practical use, which suggests the birds do it for pleasure – just as they sometimes sing because they enjoy doing so.

◀ A nightingale arrives at its nest with food for its hungry young. The young bird opens its mouth wide as a signal to the parent to feed it.

EGGS AND EGG-LAYING

▲ A female pheasant at her nest. Notice that it is built on the ground and is made of twigs, leaves and a feather or two.

◄ Within a bird's egg there is enough food to help the baby bird develop and grow. Then, when it is strong enough, it will peck a hole in the protective shell and emerge – or hatch.

Eggs

People often say something is egg-shaped. What they really mean is that it is shaped like the eggs that we use in cooking. In fact, 'egg-shaped' can be very varied. Owls lay eggs that are perfect spheres. Some birds lay longer, slimmer eggs. The eggs of others, by comparison, seem short and blunt. Most birds, however, lay eggs that are oval, but with one end more pointed than the other.

A hen bird lays her eggs in clutches. A clutch may consist of only one egg or, in the smaller birds, up to a dozen or more. All birds of the same species lay about the same number of eggs in a clutch, but when there is plenty of food the number in a clutch may double.

Most birds' eggs are coloured with spots or wavy lines, the spots and lines being usually of different colours. These colours camouflage the eggs. No two eggs in a clutch are precisely alike in colour pattern. But a few birds lay eggs that are pure white. These are usually eggs laid in a nest that is in the dark, in a cavity in a tree or in a burrow dug in a bank.

The smallest eggs are those of hummingbirds, only a few millimetres long. The largest is the ostrich egg which is 15cm (6in) long. All the birds in a species lay eggs that are roughly the same size.

The surface of eggs varies from one kind of bird to another. It may be rough, smooth or pitted. It may be polished, like shiny china, or it may be chalky, soapy or oily. Ducks and geese lay eggs with oily shells, which may have something to do with keeping the egg waterproof.

Why birds lay eggs

If an animal lays eggs it is said to be *oviparous*. If it gives birth to live young it is *viviparous*. In all classes of animals, whether they are mammals, fishes, reptiles or insects, some species are oviparous, some are viviparous. Birds are the only animals that are, without exception, oviparous. This suggests there must be a special reason for it.

As we have seen (page 9), weight is important to birds because they fly. A female cat or dog can carry her babies in her body before they are born, in spite of the extra weight, because she has four feet on the ground. The extra weight is therefore not a great burden. Birds would find flying difficult if they had to carry any extra weight. So each egg is formed within the body very quickly and then laid.

The importance to birds of being light is shown by the way that some birds, such as vultures, overeat when food is plentiful. They may then have difficulty in taking-off from the ground, which makes them easy for other birds or animals to attack. If they are chased, they have to sick up their food to lose enough weight to be able to fly.

CLASSIFYING BIRDS

Classifying animals or plants into their correct species is an extremely difficult and highly scientific task. It is also the cause of much argument and difference of opinion among scientists.

When birds are classified, scientists take much more notice of their anatomy, the bony structure of their bodies, than of their outward appearance. This is because anatomy can give many clues about how a bird has developed over millions of years. But it does produce what seem to be some very odd relations. For example, it is difficult to imagine that the kiwis and the penguins are related. But they are, and scientists have found that their skeletons are rather alike. On the other hand, hummingbirds and sunbirds look almost the same, but they are not related to each other at all. In fact hummingbirds are related to swifts and sunbirds are related to sparrows.

There are so many different species of bird that they cannot all be included in a book of this length. But as you go through the pages that follow, notice the order in which the different birds are described. They are given in their correct order, just as you would find them in the most scientific of books about birds. This order reflects the way scientists believe that the different types of bird are related to each other.

The ostrich is not only the largest living bird but was the first of the running birds known to Europeans. The Ancient Greeks knew about it and ostrich feathers have been used for personal adornment at least since medieval times. Long-legged and with a long neck, the male may be just under 240cm (8ft) tall and weigh 140kg (300lb). His body feathers are black, with white feathers in the tail and wings. The hen is slightly smaller and has dull brown feathers.

At one time ostriches were numerous in the grassy regions of Africa and northwards into Arabia and central Asia. In spite of the speed at which they could run, up to 65km (40 miles) per hour, they were hunted for their flesh and their feathers and became extinct over much of their range. In some ways the popularity of their feathers saved them, because in South Africa they were farmed especially for their feathers.

What does an ostrich eat?
The ostrich has the reputation for eating anything and swallowing hard objects, such as stones and iron nails. Its main food is, however, leaves, seeds and fruits.

Ostriches live in groups of 30 or more except in the breeding season when each cock has up to five hens, all sharing one nest, a large saucer-shaped depression in the sand in which up to 50 eggs are laid. Each egg is 15cm (6in) long and weighs over 1kg (2.2lb).

The cock and only one of the hens take turns in *incubating* the eggs, the male doing so mainly at night. When the female sits on the eggs by day, her brown plumage makes her look like a dry desert bush. She adds to this camouflage by lowering her neck until it is stretched flat on the ground, so that what would otherwise be a tall conspicuous object seems to disappear. It is this that probably gave rise to the story of ostriches burying their heads in the sand when danger threatens.

◄ A male ostrich in the Chobe Game Reserve in Botswana, southern Africa. If threatened, ostriches can run very fast.

TWO CLOSE RELATIVES

The emu

The emu which, with the kangaroo, makes up the national emblem of Australia, is the second largest living bird, after its near relative, the ostrich. Long-legged, with a long neck, its body is covered with long, limp brown feathers. The emu is unusual because it has double feathers. This means that the aftershaft (page 6) grows as long as the main shaft. Each foot has three strong toes.

Emus feed on leaves, grass and fruits and do much harm to crops, especially cereals, but they also eat large numbers of insects, especially in winter. The stomach of one emu was found to contain 3,000 caterpillars each 5cm (2in) long. They move across country in large flocks but separate into pairs for the breeding season. Each hen lays 9–20 dark green eggs in a hole scooped in the ground and lined with leaves and grass. The male incubates the eggs and protects the chicks. He goes without food and drink for two months while sitting on the eggs. The chicks are cream-coloured with long brown stripes. They stay with the parents for nearly two years.

◄ The cassowary, with its gaudy wattles, can reach a good speed even through dense jungle. It can kill a man with a thrust of the dagger-like claw on its inner toe.

The cassowary

The cassowary, another large flightless bird closely related to the emu, also lives in Australia. It lives in the northern part of the country as well as on some of the islands to the north, including New Guinea. Unlike the rather drab emu, the cassowary has bright colours on its neck and a horny *casque* on the head. Its body feathers are coarse and black. Another difference between the two birds is the long sharp claw on the inner toe of each foot. The cassowary uses it as a powerful weapon against enemies.

► The rhea is also known as the American ostrich. It lives in South America. These lesser rheas live in family groups of between 5 and 30.

THE KIWI

The kiwi is the national emblem of New Zealand, the only country in the world where the three species of kiwi are found. A flightless bird, it has smaller wings in proportion to the rest of the body than any other bird. In contrast the hen kiwi lays a bigger egg in proportion to its size than any other bird. The kiwi is, in addition, the only running bird that hunts at night and is the only bird that has its nostrils at the tip of its beak. It has poor eyesight and finds its food by smell and hearing.

A kiwi looks like a dark brown chicken and is about that size. It has no tail, however, and its beak is long, slender and flexible and used for probing the damp ground for earthworms and insects, except in summer. Then, when the ground is dry, it eats leaves and fallen fruit.

It lives in forests where there are dense growths of ferns and the soil is wet, making its simple nest in a depression in the earth between the buttress roots of trees. The male then incubates the single egg. Although it lives in places with dense vegetation the kiwi can run fast among the undergrowth to get away from danger.

▼ The drab plumage of the kiwi enables it to blend in well with the foliage and undergrowth of the forests in New Zealand where it lives.

PENGUINS

▲ Macaroni penguins breed on the small islands of the southern oceans, from the Falklands to Kerguelen in the southern Indian Ocean.

The penguin is surely the most comical of birds. It stands upright and this, with its white front, dark back and stiff wings like arms gives it a very human look. Its legs are so short that only the feet show and it can do little more than waddle about on land. In water, however, the penguin is transformed. It swims superbly, using its paddle-shaped wings as flippers, as it chases the fish which, together with prawns, are its food.

There are 17 species of penguin, and they all live in the southern hemisphere. Most of them live on islands in the southern ocean, although two actually live on the continent of Antarctica which surrounds the South Pole. The smallest, the little penguin, stands 30cm (12in) high, the largest, the emperor penguin, is 1m (3ft) high.

The females of the emperor and king penguins lay one egg a year and in the ice and snow of the Antarctic, they hold it

◄ This colony of king penguins lives on an Antarctic island. King penguins are the second largest penguin after the emperor penguin. A penguin colony is called a rookery.

► Chinstrap penguins swimming in rough seas around a rocky island. Although they are excellent swimmers, rough seas around rocky coasts take a considerable toll of old, sick or weak penguins.

on their feet to protect it from the ice and cold. It is given extra protection by a fold of belly skin that completely hides it. The males and females take it in turns to hold the egg. In regions where it is not so cold and the eggs do not have to be kept off the ground, some penguins, for example the Adélie penguins, build 'nests' of pebbles.

◄ A gentoo penguin on its nest on an island somewhere between the continent of Antarctica and the southern tip of South America. The Spaniards called it 'Juanito', a name that later became corrupted to gentoo.

WEIRD CRIES IN NORTHERN WATERS

The species of birds called divers or loons are found only in the northern hemisphere, living on rivers and lakes and in coastal waters in winter. They are probably best-known for their call, a weird, unearthly cry. The American name for them, 'loon', comes from the Old Norse name for the bird.

Divers are good swimmers and, as their name correctly suggests, good divers. They can also sink slowly in the water without causing a ripple until only the head can be seen. They swim underwater after fish, although they sometimes eat other water animals such as insects and frogs.

Long-bodied, with mostly black and white or grey *plumage*, divers or loons have thick necks, long bodies, short tails and small pointed wings. The legs with their webbed feet are set far back on the body so that, in contrast to its skill in water, a loon is awkward on land. It also has difficulty in taking to the air although once it is airborne it flies strongly.

Seen usually in ones or twos, loons nest on islands or on the shores of lakes, always near the water's edge. There, the female lays just one or two eggs in a nest that is often no more than a saucer she scraped in the ground with her feet.

◀ A great northern diver or loon sits on its nest near the edge of a lake in North America. It is also found in Greenland and Iceland.

▼ A red-throated diver incubates its eggs on a small 'island' of vegetation on a northern lake. The birds only have their distinctive red throat in the summer.

GREBES' EQUALITY OF THE SEXES

In most birds it is the male that does most, or all, of the courting. Grebes are famous for their elaborate courtship displays in which male and female play an equal part. In these displays the two birds rush at each other then meet breast-to-breast, rearing up out of the water in an upright position.

Grebes live in all parts of the world except for the polar regions. They live on ponds, lakes and rivers but will move to the sea, in coastal waters, during the winter.

Mainly grey, black or brown above, they are usually white underneath. They have short tails and long graceful necks.

In the breeding season most species grow special head feathers which they lose at the end of the season. They dive for fish and small water animals, disappearing under water with hardly a ripple and reappearing with as little fuss farther away.

The grebe's nest is a pile of weeds, floating or tethered to rushes. When disturbed, the sitting bird disappears quickly over the edge of the nest, but not before it has thrown some of the nesting material over the eggs to hide them.

▼ Great-crested grebes build large, untidy nests of water plants piled up above the level of the water.

◄ A western grebe of North America gives its baby a ride on its back. This is a common habit with other grebes, too. Swans also carry their cygnets in this way.

THE ALBATROSS – LONG DISTANCE FLIER

◄ The wandering albatross probably breeds only once in two years, because its breeding season is long. The single egg is incubated for two to three months and the young bird may take nearly a year to become adult.

► The long narrow wings of the light-mantled sooty albatross make it a superb glider. The albatross can travel long distances without beating its wings using up-draughts of wind from the waves over which it is flying to carry it along.

The main feature of an albatross is its tremendously long wings. The largest of the family is the wandering albatross which has a wingspan of nearly 4m (11½ft). Other features are the stout body, large head and strong beak, hooked at the tip to help catch their prey.

Albatrosses and their relatives, the shearwaters and petrels, are called tubenoses. The top of the bill is covered with horny plates. Under these plates are tube-like nostrils. Scientists are not certain what these odd-looking nostrils are for.

Living mainly in the southern hemisphere, albatrosses spend most of the year at sea, gliding for miles without beating their wings. They do this by using the air-currents over the waves.

Ritual 'dance'
In the breeding season they go to small islands. There they pair off and follow this with a strange courtship. The pairs grunt, cry and waddle about on stiff legs. They rub bills, bow, preen and pose with the bill pointed to the sky and their magnificent wings held out.

The nest is quite rough. Some albatross species make a scrape in the ground, others, such as the grey-headed albatross, make a mound of mud and grass. Only one egg is laid and this is incubated by the parents taking turns.

Albatrosses feed on squid and other small animals that come to the surface of the sea, mainly at night. Sometimes an albatross will follow a ship for pickings from the rubbish thrown overboard, just as gulls will do near land.

Related to albatrosses are the petrels. This name means 'little Peter'. As these small birds skim over the waves, their legs dangling, they look as if they are walking on water, like St Peter.

◄ Albatrosses only come to land to breed. This nesting colony of grey-headed albatrosses is on South Georgia, an island in the southernmost part of the Atlantic Ocean.

▼ Cory's shearwaters nest on the ground, building nests of twigs and seaweed among the rocks and stones. They lay one egg.

PELICANS

Because pelicans have short legs, it is easy to forget they are among the largest of birds, reaching 183cm (6ft). The six species live mainly in the *tropics* and two of these are found in America. They are mostly white with some black feathers in the large wings. Some species have red, orange or yellow on the large flattish bill, on the pouch and the face.

A built-in fishing net

The outstanding feature of a pelican is the large pouch underneath the beak. This is used as a fishing net. The pelican thrusts its beak into the water and the lower half opens into a scoop to catch fish. The pouch is also used for carrying food and water to the nestlings.

Pelicans live and nest in large flocks on lakes, in estuaries and on coastal *lagoons*. They also fish in groups, sweeping the shallow waters for fish, sometimes dipping their heads under the water in unison. However, one species of pelican does not fish in this way. The brown pelican of the southern United States, the West Indies, Central America and the Atlantic coast of South America from Colombia to Brazil, plunges into the sea from a height for fish, making a resounding splash on impact with the water.

Colonies of nesting birds are generally very noisy places. Pelican colonies are unusual because they are quiet, except for occasional croaks.

▼ The large, powerful wings of the brown pelican (**below**) help it take off again after it has dived into the sea to catch its food (**below centre**). These pelicans are found on the southern Atlantic coast of the USA, and the West Indies, and on the Pacific coast from British Columbia to Chile.

◀ A white pelican shows the pouch under its beak, used for catching fish. It acts as a scoop-net, as the pelican scoops it just under the surface of the water.

23

THE FISHING CORMORANTS

Cormorants can be found all over the world except for the polar regions. In fact one species, the common or great cormorant, is itself almost worldwide. All cormorants are black with a blue or green sheen to the feathers, although some species have a light throat and a few have white underparts. They breed in colonies, making bulky nests of seaweed or sticks. They hunt fish underwater, swimming with their strong webbed feet. Out of the water, they generally perch on rocks or in trees, on the coast or by lakes and rivers, with their large wings spread open to dry.

Although it cannot fly, the flightless cormorant of the Galapagos Islands still holds its small wings out when on land, perched upright in the same way as all the other cormorants.

The Guanay cormorant lives off the coast of Peru. It covers the small islands on which it nests with its droppings or guano. There is so much guano it is collected and exported as a fertilizer.

Native's fish-spearer

The darter or snakebird, a close relative of the cormorants, lives near rivers and lakes. It has a kinked neck which it uses as a spear thrower. By suddenly straightening its neck its beak is 'thrown' almost like a harpoon or spear. Fish are either caught in the beak or speared.

▲ This looks like any other cormorant but it is flightless, notice its small wings. It lives on the Galapagos Islands, and many birds that live on islands have small wings because they do not need to fly far for food.

▼ The bright red legs from which these red-legged cormorants get their name are visible in this group, perching on a cliff on the coast of South America. This kind of cormorant also has a bright yellow bill and orange face patch.

◄ The darter or snake-bird of Africa swimming. The kink in its neck makes it able to thrust out its beak with enough force to catch fish.

HERONS AND THEIR RELATIVES

There are 64 species of heron and most of them are found in warm countries, although a few live in *temperate* regions. All the species, however, look similar, with their long legs, long necks and dagger-shaped bill. They feed mainly on fish and small water animals. Their toes are long and the middle toe is used like a comb for cleaning the feathers. Their body is long and slim and the bird stands erect. The plumage is usually white but may be grey, blue, green, purple or reddish.

The plumage is loose and often includes delicate plumes as in those species known as egrets. Most herons have powder-down patches on various parts of the body. The feathers in these patches readily break up into a powder which the bird combs out and uses to remove fish slime and oil when preening.

Herons find food either by wading slowly in search of it or by standing motionless waiting for prey to swim towards them. Some, for example the African black heron, extend their wings, arching them to form an umbrella. Fish swim into the shadow cast by the wings and are caught.

An exception is the cattle egret which lives on land, seeking the company of zebras, elephants, cattle and other large mammals, feeding on the insects these disturb. Cattle egrets used to live only in Africa and southern Asia. In recent years they have surprisingly spread to the Americas and Australia.

▲ A flamingo with its chick on the muddy pile that forms the nest. Flamingoes feed in shallow water, sifting out food with their specially adapted beaks.

▼ A European bittern on the defensive. It puts on a brave show, with its beak pointed upwards, ready to attack. The bittern is a shy bird, but unlike most birds it will come forward to attack, if necessary.

▲ The broad wings, long legs and bill which are typical of herons are clearly visible in this photograph of a purple heron.

▲ The shape and markings of the male king eider's head are extremely distinctive.

There are nearly 150 different kinds of ducks, geese and swans. In spite of differences in size and colour they all look very alike and have much the same life-style. All are round-bodied, with only a short tail and a flattish bill. Some spend more time on water than others, but they all have webbed feet showing that they are water birds. Some ducks, such as wood ducks and mandarin ducks, can also

◀ Female eiders have dark mottled plumage to provide camouflage when they are sitting on their eggs. The males, in contrast appear strikingly black and white in appearance.

▼ The male mandarin duck has the most beautiful plumage of all ducks. That is why mandarins are often kept on ornamental lakes. The female is much plainer, which is the usual pattern among birds.

▶ During their courtship ritual male red-breasted mergansers half submerge themselves in the water. Mergansers have saw-edges to their bills which are useful for catching and holding fish.

perch easily on tree branches and build their nests in holes in trees. The grey-lag goose, from which the farmyard goose was bred, probably spends as much time on land as any. It feeds almost entirely on grass, although most other members of this group eat a variety of foods: grass, seeds, water plants and small animals called *crustaceans*.

In general terms, a swan is a large duck with a long neck, a goose is smaller than a swan and with a shorter neck and a duck has a shorter neck than a goose, although there is often little difference in size. For example, the Brent or Brant goose of Siberia, Greenland and northern Canada is about 58cm (23in) while the mallard of North America and north-west Europe is about 57cm ($22\frac{3}{4}$in).

Long migrations

Many members of this group of birds live in the far north and make long *migrations* each year. As the weather gets colder in their northern breeding grounds ducks, geese and swans fly south to areas where the ground is not frozen or snow-covered and food is still available. Often they fly in large V-shaped formations, covering great distances each day before coming down to feed and rest. There are, however, records of non-stop migrations. A flock of blue and snow geese travelled from James Bay in Canada to Louisiana, a distance of 2,700km (1,678 miles) in 60 hours or about 1,100km (684 miles) a day. Even more remarkable is the record of ducks migrating from Manitoba to Louisiana. They covered a distance of 2,400km (1,490 miles) at the rate of about 1,800km (1,118 miles) a day.

▼ A family of Canada geese, with ten goslings. Native of North America, this swan-like goose has been introduced into Europe, where it is now very common in places.

▶ A mute swan comes in to land. Despite their name, these swans will hiss and snort when angry.

▼ These black-necked swans live in South America. The cob (male) and the pen (female) are each carrying a cygnet (young swan) on its back.

▶ The whooper swan is named for its bugle-like double call. It lives in northern Europe and Siberia, coming south in winter to warmer climates.

VULTURES

▲ An Egyptian vulture perches on a dead animal. Its hooked beak, typical of vultures, shows very clearly.

Vultures are a kind of bird-of-prey, as large as eagles. The difference between vultures and eagles is that a vulture does not kill healthy animals unless they are very small. If a vulture sees an animal that is sick or dying it comes down and waits for it to die then feeds on its flesh.

There are two kinds of vulture: the *Old World* vultures and the *New World* vultures. The first kind includes the lammergeier and also the palm-nut vulture, which feeds on nuts of the oil-palm. The New World vultures include the condors.

Both kinds look much alike. They are large birds – the lammergeier has a wingspan of 2.7m (9ft). Some species, for example the Californian condor, have a head and neck almost naked except for a layer of fine down.

The reason for flying high

Vultures spend much of their time soaring on air-currents for hours at altitudes of up to 6,000m (20,000ft), looking out for dead or dying animals. By flying at a great height, vultures, like

other birds-of-prey, can watch a huge area. When they see something to eat, they travel very fast: they have to reach it before it is completely devoured by other animals and birds.

▼ The black vulture of Spain and Portugal is now a rare bird. It has been shot and poisoned. Also, there are not so many animal carcases left lying around these days.

◀ The Andean condor is a kind of vulture and largest of all birds-of-prey, with a wing-span of over 3m (10ft). It lives in the Andes mountains of South America. Some vultures are naked on the head and neck so when delving into a carcase their feathers are not spoilt.

◄ Head of a golden eagle, showing the hooked beak used to tear the flesh of its prey.

▼ A tawny or steppe eagle perching on a branch with a small bird it has just caught. These eagles live in open country from Romania east to India.

The term 'bird-of-prey' is used to describe birds that kill and eat other animals. Birds-of-prey form a group that includes eagles, hawks, falcons, buzzards and kites. There are other birds, such as shrikes and gulls, that kill animals for food, but birds-of-prey are particularly noted for it. They all have hooked beaks and strong toes ending in stout claws or *talons*.

Skilful fliers

All birds-of-prey are excellent fliers – they must be, because they depend on their ability to fly fast and manoeuvre swiftly to catch their prey. The large birds-of-prey, such as eagles have broad wings with a span of 2m (6½ft). Like vultures, the larger birds-of-prey fly high in the sky, observing a wide area for the possibility of food. They use air currents, or *thermals*, to carry them and if you are lucky enough to see a buzzard or an eagle soaring, you will see how seldom they flap their wings.

The smallest of this group of birds are the pygmy falcons which are only about 21cm (8½in) long – that is about the same size as a starling. These small birds-of-

prey feed entirely on insects caught in the air. The largest are the eagles with their massive wing-spans. The falcons have long pointed wings and are especially swift in flight. They generally catch their prey by swooping or *stooping* on them as they fly, capturing them after a swift dive. Sometimes they reach speeds of 160km (100 miles) per hour as they stoop.

▼ A black-winged kite on its nest. Although each pair of black-winged kites builds a new nest each year, the nests are often in the same tree.

▼ The caracara of the Americas belongs to the birds-of-prey known as falcons.

▶ The secretary bird of the grasslands of southern Africa builds its nest in the top of a low tree.

► An osprey perches on a tree-top with the prey it has just caught.

▼ Red-footed falcons live principally on insects, so migrate southwards when colder weather reduces their food supply in the northern parts of Russia and central Asia.

Birds under threat

Birds-of-prey are everywhere more scarce than they used to be. Because they sometimes kill poultry and animals, such as lambs, they have been mercilessly shot, trapped or poisoned. Modern agricultural methods have also played a part and as more land is cultivated there is less habitat for the birds. The bald eagle, the national symbol of the United States, is now fairly rare except in remote parts of Alaska. But some of the smaller falcons, the European kestrel, for example, have adapted to life in modern cities – the tall buildings provide excellent nesting sites.

► Although the bald eagle is the national emblem of the United States this did not save it from the hunter and it is now scarce. Its name is misleading because it is not bald. Its head and neck are white and this makes it look bald. Although it kills birds, its main food is fish.

Many birds-of-prey, including the peregrine (**left**), are threatened by deliberate killing, poisoning from eating prey killed with powerful chemicals, and a decreasing area in which to live as cities grow and land is cleared for farming.

Even if an adult bird is not killed by eating poisoned prey, the chemicals in the poison can still affect the birds. The females may lay thin-shelled eggs (**below**) in which the chick cannot survive and develop.

GAMEBIRDS

◄ The male sage grouse courting, seen from the front. Its head is thrown back and the white ruff on the neck is puffed out.

common is that although they can fly, more often than not they walk or run. Their strong legs and strong toes are used for scratching over earth as they search for their food of seeds and insects.

The male of most kinds of gamebird usually has strong spurs on his legs for fighting and also has very bright feathers. On his head he has coloured folds of naked skin, called *wattles*. These vary according to the species – think of the difference in the wattles of the turkey and a farmyard cockerel.

▼ A male ptarmigan in his white winter plumage is hard to see against the snow. This natural camouflage helps protect it from its enemies. In summer the ptarmigan's plumage changes to mottled brown, making the bird almost invisible among the grass, as long as it stays still.

Many birds are used as food and are hunted or shot, but there are some which are especially hunted for sport. These are known as gamebirds. The first ever to be hunted in this way was the jungle fowl of India. This was also the first to be domesticated, over 3,000 years ago, and is the bird we now know as the farmyard chicken.

Pheasants

Closely related to the jungle fowl is the pheasant. This came from south-west Asia. The Romans fattened it in special pens for use at their feasts. They took it all over Europe with them as they conquered tribe after tribe to form their great empire 2,000 years ago, although it does not seem to have reached Britain until brought by the Normans in the eleventh century. The pheasants adapted well to their new surroundings and became semi-wild.

Turkeys

The first European settlers in America found the turkey very enjoyable to eat, and took it back to Europe. It is now often the main dish of a meal on festive occasions such as Thanksgiving Day and Christmas Day.

The turkey belongs to the same family as the pheasant and the jungle fowl. So do the peacock, the guinea fowl and the grouse. One thing these birds have in

▲ The cock common pheasant has striking head markings. Originally from south-west Asia, these pheasants are now popular gamebirds in many parts of the world.

► A male prairie chicken of North America showing off its feathers as it courts a female.

BRUSH TURKEYS – 'THE BIG FEET'

▼ The black and white maleo fowl lives on the island of Celebes in south-east Asia. It is one of the group of birds known as brush turkeys.

The first white settlers in Australia were puzzled by large mounds of earth. They thought these must be burial mounds made by the Aborigines. The truth came out later. These mounds, the largest of which were 2m (6½ft) high, 13m (40ft) across and containing 12 tonnes or more of earth, were made by birds known as megapodes, meaning big feet. Other names since given to the birds include mound-builders, brush turkeys and mallee fowl.

Nests with a difference

The mounds proved to be nests, but with a difference. They were also incubators. As the breeding season draws near the males dig a deep pit with their strong feet. They scrape dead leaves and plants from all around to fill the pit. Then they cover this with a thick layer of sand. The rotting leaves and plants become very hot, like the compost heaps that gardeners make.

After a while the heap cools off. When it has reached the right temperature the males allow the females to lay their eggs in it. From September to April the males tend the heap, keeping it at the right temperature so that the eggs get neither too cold nor too hot. To do this they test the heap with their beaks, using their tongues as thermometers, to keep the temperature at 33°C (92°F). That is, just below your own blood heat. Should the temperature rise too much, they open up the heap to let the heat escape.

Brush turkeys are found in Australia, New Guinea and other islands of the South Pacific, as far north as the Philippines. In some places the nests are made in hot volcanic sand. But it is always the males that keep the mounds at an even temperature.

▼ The brown-collared brush turkey of Papua-New Guinea.

▲ Brush turkey from Papua-New Guinea, showing the strong feet it uses to build the mounds that incubate its eggs.

THE DANCING CRANES

Cranes and storks look very similar. Both kinds of bird have long legs and long necks, the tallest, the Sarus crane of southern Asia, is 1.5m (5ft). But the bill of a crane is not as long as a stork's. Most cranes have beautiful plumage: mainly white, grey and pale browns. One species, the crowned crane, has a crest of feathers on its head, from which it gets its name.

Spectacular dancers
Cranes are best known for their courtship dances. The birds walk with quick steps and outstretched wings, bowing their heads and jumping in the air, then suddenly stopping. Sometimes a pair will dance together, sometimes a whole group will go through the steps together, often continuing until they are exhausted. As they dance they call loudly. In some cranes the call is more of a whistle but in others it is like a trumpet being blown. The windpipe of a trumpeting crane is long and coiled, like the tube of a trumpet. The coils are lodged in the bird's hollow bones, especially in a hollow in the breastbone.

Cranes live in large flocks and spend most of the time on the ground. However, they are good fliers. They fly in V-formations with the neck outstretched, trumpeting as they go. Sadly, many of the 14 species of cranes are threatened with extinction. For example there are now about 100 whooping cranes and about 1,200 Japanese or red-crowned cranes. Cranes mainly live in wetlands – marshy ground and reed beds – or else live in *arid* areas but return to damp areas to breed. Each year more of the Earth's wetlands are reclaimed for farming, so reducing the areas where cranes can live and breed.

▲ The most showy of all cranes are the African crowned cranes. They are famous also for their dancing in the breeding season.

WADERS OR SHORE-BIRDS

▼ The marsh sandpiper uses its long bill to probe in shallow water and mud for its food: water-insects and their larvae, and molluscs.

▲ A group of waders on a rocky island near the coast in Europe. They include knots, redshanks (grey with red legs) and oyster-catchers or sea-pies, black-and-white, with legs and bill red.

Wherever land and water meet, except where there is ice, you will be likely to see waders or shore-birds. They may be in ones or twos or in large flocks, on the seashore, in estuaries or lakes, or on marshes or moors. In fact, wherever the ground is soft.

Most waders have long legs and a long bill. The largest of them look like small storks. Whether large or small, waders feed by probing sand, mud or soft earth for small animals, such as insects and worms, or else they pick them off the surface.

Their plumage is usually what scientists describe as cryptic. That is, it is coloured in browns and greys which make the birds difficult to see so long as they are still.

Long-distance fliers
Many shore-birds migrate long distances between their nesting places and the places where they spend the winter. The whimbrel, for example, breeds in the far north of Europe and Russia and spends the winter in west Africa, south of the Sahara desert. The solitary sandpiper,

which breeds in Canada and Alaska, winters in Central and South America. These long journeys often make the birds easy targets for hunters. The eskimo curlew once bred in large numbers in the *tundra* in northern Canada. It spends the winters in Chile, Argentina and Uruguay, and in making these long journeys almost up and down the length of the American continent it was hunted so much that it is almost extinct. Shore-birds' nests are hard to find. Although little more than a scrape in the ground, the eggs and chicks are beautifully camouflaged to match the surrounding sand and stones. The parent birds may also lure enemies away from the nest by flapping their wings and calling loudly.

GULLS AND TERNS

Gulls

We usually call them seagulls, although scientists prefer to call them just 'gulls'. Although they are seen at sea they are usually not far from land. A gull may follow a ship going out to sea but very soon the bird will turn back. Also, many gulls spend almost all their time flying over land and resting on lakes and rivers. And, of course, they breed and feed on land.

There is a famous monument as far inland as Salt Lake City, in the United States. In the middle of the nineteenth century a plague of grasshoppers looked like destroying the crops of the people who had just settled there. The crops were saved by the arrival of flocks of Franklin's gulls and California gulls. These ate the insects.

In many parts of the world gulls do a service by feeding on the garbage heaps found near towns. They also eat refuse floating at sea. Indeed, a gull will eat almost anything. They will follow fishing vessels to snap up the fish guts thrown overboard and they will also catch fish swimming near the surface. In fact gulls are largely *scavengers* and will eat flesh off carcasses of dead animals lying on the ground or floating at sea. They also kill young birds and rob nests of their eggs.

Gulls nest in colonies. Those that spend most of the year inland migrate to the coasts and build their nests on damp meadows or on cliffs.

Terns

Terns are close relatives of the gulls. Sometimes terns are called sea-swallows because of their forked tails. They, like the gulls, are mainly white but are grey or black on the wings and tail. They live not far out to sea, feeding on fish swimming near the surface. Terns also nest in colonies.

One kind, the Arctic tern, is famous for making the longest migration of any animal. It breeds in the Arctic. Then it flies south to the Antarctic for the southern summer, a distance of 17,703km (11,000 miles) each way.

◀ Heermann's gull lives on the Pacific coast of the United States. It has a white head and dark neck and body plumage.

▲ The herring gull is common and widespread throughout the northern hemisphere. Like other gulls it will eat almost anything, but is noted for following shoals of herring swimming close to the surface of the sea.

◀ The long beak and forked swallow-like tail of this elegant tern are typical of most kinds of tern.

PIGEONS AND DOVES

▲ Crowned pigeons of New Guinea are large and have a crown of lace-like feathers. They live in forests and feed on fruits, seeds and insects.

▼ A turtle dove at its nest with its young ones. Soon it will be giving them another feed of pigeon's milk.

There is no real difference between the birds we call pigeons and those we call doves, except that the smaller kinds are usually called doves. The domestic pigeon, the one you can see in most towns and cities, is also called the rock dove. Pigeons and doves are found all over the world except near the poles. They range in size from the diamond dove which is 15cm (6in) long to the Victoria crowned pigeon of New Guinea, which is a large bird about 84cm (33in) long. This pigeon has beautiful blue plumage and a splendid crown of feathers. At the beginning of this century the bird was hunted for these feathers which were used, like those of the birds-of-paradise (page 60), to decorate hats for the rich and fashionable.

Whether they are called pigeons or doves they are all alike, with plump, rounded bodies and small heads. Their legs are short and most of them coo or croon, although a few make booming calls. The gentle cooing of the turtle dove has inspired poets in the same way that the song of the lark (page 50) has done. Sometimes, in an old poem, you may read of 'the voice of the turtle'. The poet really means the voice of the turtle dove, not the turtle that lives in the sea.

Pigeons and doves live in flocks, spending their time in trees except when feeding. Their food is mainly seeds, berries and buds, but some eat small snails and insects. In the *tropics* there are many kinds of fruit-eating pigeons. The Victoria crowned pigeon is one of them. To drink pigeons dip their beaks into water and suck. They do not raise their heads to swallow the water as most other birds do.

A bird that produces milk?
The way pigeons and doves feed their young is also unusual. Both parents produce 'pigeon's milk' in their crops. This is a liquid which is rich in protein and is used for feeding the young. The young pigeon, which is known as a *squab*, feeds by putting its head in the parent's mouth and taking the milk.

◄ The plumed pigeon is a native of Australasia. Its brown body plumage is barred with black and there is a stiff little plume of feathers on its head.

PARROTS

The parrot family is a large one, made up of over 300 species of parrakeets, parrotlets, macaws, amazons, lovebirds, budgerigars, rosellas, lories, lorikeets and three New Zealand parrots known as the kea, the kaka and the kakapo or owl-parrot. The smallest are some of the lovebirds which are only 10cm (4in) long, and the largest are the macaws which may be just over 1m (40in) long.

Some parrots have short tails, others long. Yct all are much alike in having bright feathers and short, hooked beaks. Their legs, too, are short. The feet have four toes, two pointing forward and two back. Parrots live in trees where they climb, using their feet to grasp the branches and using the beak as a third 'hand'. They also use their feet to take food to their mouths.

Parrots lay their eggs in holes in trees, in spaces among rocks or in holes in sandbanks. The nest is very simple, usually no more than a layer of wood chips.

Birds of many voices

They are noisy birds, the voices of the larger species being a harsh screech. When kept as pets they become expert mimics of all manner of sounds. They imitate human words and will even sing songs. It was this, and their intelligence, that made them favourites with the Ancient Romans, who were the first to keep African parrots as pets nearly 2,000 years ago. It is also this ability to mimic that gives us our expression 'parrot-fashion', when someone repeats without thinking what other people have said.

▲ The red fan parrot lives in tropical rain forests.

◄ The sulphur-crested cockatoo is found in Australia.

► Scarlet macaws and red and green macaws are two of the largest members of the parrot family. They live in the tropical forests of South America.

CUCKOOS IN THE NEST

▼ A newly hatched European cuckoo has shouldered the eggs of its foster-parent out of the nest. It is just tipping out the last egg.

▼ The roadrunner, or chaparral cock, lives in the southern United States. It is related to he European cuckoo but runs rather than flies. And it is not a nest-parasite. It hatches its own eggs and feeds its own chicks, instead of getting other birds to do this.

A few birds live by robbing other birds of their food. They are called *parasites*. A few more lay their eggs in the nests of other birds. The real owners of the nests then have the task of rearing the young birds when they hatch. These are known as *nest-parasites*. The most famous is the European cuckoo. This bird spends the winter in Africa, migrating to Europe for the summer to breed. Most species of American cowbird also lay their eggs in the nests of smaller birds. This means that the female cuckoo or cowbird does not have to work hard building a nest or spend days incubating the eggs. Nor does she have to spend hours each day feeding her baby after it has hatched. Once the young intruder has hatched it will push the other eggs or young out of the nest. The young cuckoo even has a special hollow in its back to make this task of heaving the egg out easier. If you wonder why the birds whose nest it really is do not recognize the cuckoo's egg, it is because the cuckoo's egg often looks very like the 'proper' eggs.

Not all members of the cuckoo family are nest-parasites, the North American species build their own nests. And members of other families are nest-parasites. One is the black-headed duck of South America. It lays its eggs in the nests of other ducks. And the honey-guides of Africa lay their eggs in barbets' and woodpeckers' nests.

▼ The common cuckoo has a very wide range: it breeds from Ireland in the west across central Europe and Asia to Japan in the east. To avoid the cold northern winters, this species of cuckoo migrates south to southern Asia and tropical Africa.

▲ A half-grown European cuckoo in the tiny nest in which it was reared by a small foster-parent. Birds that have the misfortune to have a cuckoo's egg laid in their nest must work hard to feed the young cuckoo which is so much larger than their own young would have been.

OWLS

Owls can be found almost everywhere in the world, from the cold Arctic tundra to the hot plains of Africa. They also range in size from the tiny sparrow-like pygmy owls and the elf owls only 14cm (5½in) to the large eagle owls which are about 71cm (28in) long. But whatever their size, owls all look alike. They have a rounded body, a large head, a short tail and large eyes. We think they look wise because their eyes are directed forwards, as ours are. Indeed, with their short hooked beak, an owl's face can look very human.

Silent hunters

Like eagles and hawks (page 30), owls are birds-of-prey and have powerful talons for catching small birds and animals. The main difference is that owls usually hunt by night. To do this they need good night vision and owls can see far better in the dark than you can. They also have excellent hearing, and can fly down and catch a mouse in total darkness, using only their ears. Most owls hunt at night and as well as good sight and hearing they have fluffy feathers. These deaden the noise of their wings, so that the owl's victims cannot hear it coming.

Because they usually rest by day owls must hide from enemies. So their plumage is camouflaged, which means it is mainly brown and grey, to make them very hard to see. The snowy owl of the Arctic is an exception – it is white. However, the female, which sits on the nest, is striped for camouflage.

▼ Most owls are nocturnal birds – roosting by day and hunting at night. The fairly short, rounded wings help the owl fly easily among woodland trees.

◀ The barn owl is the best-known of all owls. It is found almost worldwide. It feeds on mice and rats and makes its nest in buildings.

▼ Unlike most owls, little owls can quite often be seen during the day.

NIGHTJARS

► The common nighthawk of America sits resting on the ground. The shading and patterning of its feathers make it hard to see while it stays still.

▼ The common European nightjar is also well camouflaged. At sunset the male flies up to a perch. There it calls to its mate, making a harsh churring sound. It goes on calling throughout the night.

Nightjars get their name because they fly at night and they also make a jarring or churring sound, like a stick being run along wooden fence slats. In the United States they are often called nighthawks because they hunt for insects after dark. They are also called goatsuckers because there is a legend that these birds suck milk from goats. It probably began because the birds were seen near goats, but most likely they were really after insects.

The nightjar's camouflaged plumage, mottled in shades of buff, brownish-red, grey and black, also helps to keep it hidden. During the day a nightjar or nighthawk rests on the ground. Its colours blend so perfectly with the grass and leaves around it that it is almost impossible to see.

The bird hunts insects on the wing, catching them in its large gaping mouth.

North American species of nightjar include the well-known whip-poor-will, so named because when it calls that is what it seems to be saying. Another is the poor-will, famous because it is the only bird known to *hibernate* during the winter.

SWIFTS

Centuries ago it was said that swifts roosted in the heavens. Another legend was that if they landed on the ground they could not take off again. Both are nearly true: swifts rarely land on the ground, and although they can take off again, they do not find it very easy.

Always in the air

Swifts are almost always in the air. They feed in the air. They mate in the air. They even drink on the wing, flying over water and dropping down to take a sip. And except when they have young in the nest, the common swifts fly higher and higher as darkness falls until they are out of sight. They are believed to spend the night in the air.

They are about 16.5cm (6½in) long, which is much the same size as a swallow, but swifts have longer wings that are narrow, pointed and curved. The birds are superb fliers, moving fast and skilfully between and around buildings in towns and cities.

Nature's weather forecaster

Swifts are very sensitive to electric storms. When a thunderstorm is brewing they can be seen flying in a stream along a course at right angles to that of the storm. They may fly several hundred kilometres away from the path of a storm and may not return for several days. If it is during the nesting season and they are feeding young ones these do not starve. Instead they go into a type of hibernation until the parents return and start feeding them again.

Swifts nest in hollow trees, in holes in cliffs or in buildings, in the spaces under the roofs. The chimney swift of North America nests, as the name suggests, in chimneys. Unlike most other swifts which have a forked tail, the chimney swift's tail has a blunt, squared-off end. There is a small swift in south-east Asia that builds nests of its own saliva high up on the walls of caves. These nests are collected and cooked for making birds'-nest soup.

▼ Swifts very, very rarely land on the ground but will sometimes cling, like this one, to a vertical surface, just for a few moments. They are able to cling like this because the four toes on each foot all point forwards.

HUMMINGBIRDS – NATURE'S JEWELS

All hummingbirds are small and have a long slender bill. The smallest, the bee hummingbird, is no bigger than a bumblebee, 5cm (2in) long. The largest, the giant hummingbird, is 21cm (8½in) and that includes the long beak.

Hummingbirds are the most brightly coloured of all birds, with their brilliantly metallic and iridescent scale-like feathers. All day long they flit among the brightly coloured flowers of tropical America, sipping nectar or catching tiny insects. For this, they use their long tongue like a double tube. Most of them hover in front of a flower, beating their oar-shaped wings so fast that they make a humming sound.

If a hummingbird lands on the ground it will be unable to walk, because its legs are small and weak. In contrast, the breast muscles, which are so important for flying, make up 30 per cent of the bird's whole weight.

The hummingbird lays the smallest of all birds' eggs. Each one is less than 13mm (½in).

▲ The black-bellied thorntail is one of the hummingbird family. These birds occur only on the American continent, ranging from Alaska to Tierra del Fuego, although they are most common in the tropical areas.

▲ The jewel-like feathers of hummingbirds make people give these birds fancy names. This one, on a perch in a zoo, is called the golden-tailed sapphire.

◀ The female broadbilled hummingbird of North America perches on her flimsy nest. She is about to feed her chicks. These hummingbirds never lay more than two eggs.

▲ A hummingbird, known as Anna's hummingbird, hovering in front of a flower. As it hovers it pushes its long bill into the flower to suck nectar.

KINGFISHERS AND THEIR RELATIVES

Kingfishers are dumpy birds with brilliant plumage. They have short tails and strong dagger-like beaks and most of them live near rivers or lakes. Their main food is small fish, but they also eat water insects, tadpoles and frogs, diving into the water for them. Some kingfishers also eat snakes and lizards.

There are 87 different kinds of kingfisher, most of which live in south-east Asia. The most widespread is the common kingfisher found throughout Europe, in Africa and as far east as the Solomon Islands.

Kingfishers vary in size quite considerably. The pygmy kingfisher is about 10cm (4in) long, while the giant African kingfisher is 45cm (18in) long. A few species live well away from water and are called forest kingfishers. The best known of these is the Australian kookaburra, or laughing jackass.

The fishing kingfishers make their nests in river banks hacking a tunnel into the soil with their beaks. At the end of the tunnel they excavate a chamber in which the eggs are laid. The forest kingfishers make their nests in holes in trees.

Relatives of the kingfishers
The kingfishers have over 100 different species related to them. Most of these also have bright plumage. They include the todies, motmots, bee-eaters, rollers, hoopoes and hornbills.

▼ The brilliantly coloured kingfisher of Europe on its look-out perch. It has just come back from diving into the river to catch a fish.

▲ Wood-hoopoes are also related to kingfishers. They live among trees in tropical Africa, feeding on insects they find in crevices in the bark.

◄ The laughing jackass or kookaburra is an Australian forest kingfisher. It does not need water to find its food. It catches insects in the air or picks them up from the ground.

WOODPECKERS

The green woodpecker of Europe is also called the yaffle, from its laughing call. It chisels a chamber in an old tree in which to lay its eggs. It feeds on insects hacked out of the wood or digs out ants living in the ground.

As you walk through woodland, birds will fly up as you draw near. Most of them fly into trees and perch. But if you are lucky enough to see a woodpecker, notice how it flies to the nearest tree and clings to the trunk, holding itself there with its strong toes. The ends of its tail feathers also help. They are like stiff spikes and dig into the bark, acting as a prop.

A natural wood-cutter

A woodpecker needs this help when it is feeding. It has to hold on while striking the tree trunk with its chisel-like beak. This is the way it bores into wood. Then it inserts its long sticky tongue into the hole to catch the insects tunnelling through the wood.

Woodpeckers also need to chisel into wood for their nests. A pair will select a place on a tree trunk and hack a hole into it. Then they chip away until there is quite a large cavity in which to lay the eggs and bring up their young. Woodpeckers are climbers from birth. Young woodpeckers can climb about in their nests inside trees before they are able to fly.

If you bang your head against something hard it hurts and you may even get a headache. A really hard knock can cause brain damage. But woodpeckers cannot live without striking their beaks against something hard, whether to feed or to make nests. To prevent damage to their brains woodpeckers' beaks are specially adapted where they join the skull so that the brain is not jarred and damaged.

◀ Woodpeckers, such as this grey-headed woodpecker, use their strong, stiff tail feathers to provide extra support as they search for food on tree trunks.

OVENBIRDS

◀ The white-eyed foliage-gleaner of South America feeds on insects and spiders it finds among dead leaves.

The most important things for a bird building its nest are that it should be warm and secure. The ovenbird of tropical South America has solved these problems by building what looks like a mud oven.

The ovenbird itself is not much to look at. It is about the size of a thrush, appproximately 23cm (9in) long, and is reddish brown with a white front. Its nest, on the other hand, is eye-catching. It is built on a tree branch or a fence, often near a house, as if to show the bird is unafraid of people, and looks like a mud hut with an opening to one side. This 'door' leads into a passage-way in which is another 'door' leading into the nest chamber itself.

Day after day, while building their nest, a pair of ovenbirds carry pellets of soft red clay to build the walls and then roof it over. The walls are nearly 4cm (1½in) thick and once dried even a tropical downpour will not hurt it. Inside, the eggs and young birds are also safe from enemies.

▲ The ovenbird of South America builds a nest of mud. It is shaped like the ovens once used by peasants for baking bread.

◀ The stripe-breasted spinetail, another type of South American ovenbird, lives both in dense rain forests and more open grasslands.

47

LYREBIRDS

The first scientists to see the lyrebird, at the end of the eighteenth century, were puzzled: they did not know what to call it or how to classify it. Some called it the native pheasant. Others called it the New South Wales bird-of-paradise. Not until 20 years later was it called a lyrebird and it was the tail that gave it its name. This is because the tail of the male is made up of 14 wire-like feathers and two broader feathers. Very occasionally the tail is erected and for a moment it looks like a lyre. This is how it is shown on Australian stamps. Generally, the bird brings its tail feathers forward over its head, like an umbrella.

A natural mimic

The hen lyrebird starts to build a nest in the forests of south-east Australia in May or June, in mid-winter. The nest is on a large pile of sticks and has a roof of moss. The hen lays one egg which she broods for six weeks. Throughout this time the male builds up to ten low platforms of sticks. These platforms are 1m (3ft) across. He goes from one platform to another, singing on each platform. He also imitates the songs of other birds, as well as imitating mechanical sounds, such as the rattling of chains and the sound of a saw.

▲ The beautiful lyrebird of Australia is hard to see until it spreads its tail. Its plumage is a dull brown, which makes good camouflage against the forest floor.

► The male lyrebird spreads his tail when showing off to his hen. He then shimmers the lace-like feathers to attract her attention.

THE NOISY SCRUB-BIRD

There is at least one bird that has beaten the wren at being heard but not seen. At about 15cm (6in) it is a little bigger than the wren and lives only in Australia. The Australian Aborigines knew it and called it *Jee-mul-uk*. The white settlers did not find it until 1842 and named it the noisy scrub-bird, because it has such a loud voice. It is also an excellent mimic and imitates the songs of other birds.

It spends its time on the ground, feeding on insects. It is a poor flyer although it can run fast. A few were caught and sent to museums in Australia, Britain and the United States. Little more was known about it when, in 1889, it seemed to be extinct. A memorial was erected to commemorate both the bird and John Gilbert, the scientist who first found it.

A happy return

To everyone's surprise, the bird turned up again in 1961. Two years later, in south-west Australia, the first nest was found. It was a round nest, built of dry leaves, close to the ground in long grass. Fortunately, this bird with the loud voice, had not been killed off after all. It is now protected by law. But the amazing thing is: how did such a noisy bird escape detection for three-quarters of a century?

About 2,500 miles away, in New South Wales, another species of scrub-bird, the rufous scrub-bird, has been found. It, too, was very few in numbers.

Scientists believe that these two species, so far from each other on the Australian continent, are the only survivors of a family of birds that was once very common throughout Australia.

▼ Scrub-birds live in Australia, in dense undergrowth. They are shy and keep out of sight. In contrast, their voices are loud, so they are often heard but seldom seen.

49

LARKS – MAGNIFICENT SONGSTERS

► A female greater red-breasted meadowlark perches on a bush in southern Argentina.

There are over 70 different kinds of lark, but only one of these, the horned lark, is found in America. No other birds has so caught the attention of poets as the European skylark. Shakespeare wrote: 'Hark! the lark at Heaven's gate sings'. The poet Coleridge spoke of the lark as 'an angel in the clouds', and composers have tried to capture, in music, the beauty of the lark's song.

In fact the poetry and music celebrate the male skylark's habit of rising from the ground on fluttering wings, singing as it goes higher and higher until it is almost out of sight. The horned lark also does this. And both species also sing when perched on a stone or a post. Whether singing in the air or on the ground, all members of the lark family are exquisite songsters.

Carefully hidden nests

Although larks' songs are so beautiful, and the birds are easy to see as they fly upwards, singing loudly, once on the ground it is a different matter. Few birds blend so well with their surroundings and are so difficult to see. Patterned, speckled, spotted and streaked in a variety of browns, the skylark also hides its nest from prying eyes in a similar way. The nest is a few pieces of grass in a depression in the ground. The 4–5 eggs are blotched and speckled so that they are almost invisible on the open pasture where they are laid. In fact, scientists have discovered that larks in Africa and the Middle East are patterned slightly differently according to the soil in the area where the larks live. In areas of dark volcanic soil, the larks are much darker than larks living in areas where the soil is sandy.

▲ Fischer's finch-lark of Africa has a much heavier, more finch-like beak than the crested lark (**left**).

◄ A crested lark of Europe returns to feed its nestlings. The cup-shaped nest built in a tussock of grass is very hard to see without a great deal of searching.

50

SIGNS OF SUMMER

◀ House martins gather in large flocks on roofs and telephone wires before starting their journey south to warmer countries for the winter. These gatherings of martins are a sign that summer is coming to an end.

Swallows

One of the best-known birds, certainly in the northern hemisphere, is the beautiful summer visitor known as the barn swallow in North America and as the swallow in Europe. Its arrival each year is a sign that winter is over, although there are many old country sayings, such as 'One swallow doesn't make a summer', to indicate that there may still be cold weather ahead. In the southern hemisphere an Australian species of swallow migrates southwards and is known as the welcome swallow.

Martins

Martins are close relatives of swallows. Indeed, the bird known as the sand martin in Britain is called the bank swallow in North America.

Swallows and martins are small birds, usually dark on the back, white on the front, with forked tails. They spend the day flying swiftly back and forth high in the air, snapping up small flying insects. At night, during the breeding season, they roost in their cup-shaped nests made of pellets of mud, stuck together with saliva from their mouths. At other times they roost in flocks, in dense vegetation.

They seldom land on the ground except to collect mud for the nest from around the edge of a pond or puddle. And if you ever see any doing this you will understand why. These birds that fly so beautifully and make long migrations each year are at a great disadvantage once they are on the ground. Their legs are short and weak, and their feet, so suitable for gripping the edge of their nest to feed their young, are not designed for walking easily on the ground.

▼ A swallow at its nest of mud on the rafter of a barn. It feeds its young on insects it catches on the wing.

THE LOUD-VOICED WREN

Some birds are often heard but seldom seen. One bird of which this is true is the Jenny wren. It is found throughout Asia, Europe and North Africa, as well as North America, where it is called the winter wren.

There are many kinds of wrens living in America. The Jenny wren, or winter wren, migrated from there and spread over the rest of the northern hemisphere. Small, dapper, with its tail cocked perkily, it has also been called 'the small bird with the big voice'. Hidden in a bush, it pauses in its search for insects and spiders, to pour out a torrent of song.

The feathered cave-dweller
This wren is a troglodyte, a cave-dweller, when it comes to building a nest. (In fact the wren's scientific name is *Troglodytes*

troglodytes.) Anything looking like a cave will do for a nesting place. It may be a garden shed, a hollow tree, under an overhanging bank or in a mass of ivy. Even an old kettle, teapot or empty can blown into a hedge may hold a wren's nest. The male builds several nests. The hen chooses one of them and adds a lining. In it she lays her eggs. The other nests, without a lining, are not used. They are called cocks' nests.

Apart from the true wrens, like the winter wren and Jenny wren, there are a number of small brown birds elsewhere in the world called wrens. There are, for example, Australian and New Zealand wrens, such as the riflewren and fernwren, but these are not true wrens, merely small plump brownish birds that look rather like wrens.

▼ One of the smallest birds in Europe is the common wren. It is also one of the best at keeping out of sight, although it often gives itself away with its loud voice.

▲ The house wren of North America, like the European wren (**left**), lives in dense undergrowth often remarkably close to roads and houses.

MOCKINGBIRDS

◀ The catbird of North America is another of the mockingbirds. It miaows like a cat, but not in imitation of a cat. It is its natural call.

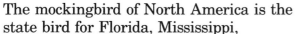

▲ The brown thrasher, cousin to the mockingbird, sitting on its nest. It calls in loud melodious whistles and also mimics the songs of other birds.

The mockingbird of North America is the state bird for Florida, Mississippi, Tennessee, Arkansas and Texas. There is also an old song that starts 'Listen to the mockingbird', which suggests that there is something special about this bird's song – and so there is.

The bird itself is not much to look at. The size of a thrush, it has a long tail and short rounded wings. It keeps close to the ground, even building its nest low down in a bush.

It has a loud and varied song. There are so many different notes in it that some people believed the mockingbird could imitate every bird around – and that is how it got its name. Moreover, when scientists came to study the mockingbird they found that, although it does sometimes imitate the songs of other birds, it is not as good a mimic as people had thought. Nevertheless, it does imitate the sounds made by other birds, so it is fun to watch quietly one of these birds and try to identify the birds it is imitating. You can do the same with starlings, and they are even better mimics.

THRUSHES – A FAMILY OF SINGERS

There are about 300 different kinds of thrush, and one of the most notable features of the family is the number of thrushes that have beautiful songs. One of the sweetest songs is that of the European song thrush, a brown bird with a pale speckled breast. Closely related to it, and another fine singer, is the blackbird. Only the male is black although its beak is yellow or orange. The female is brown with some speckling on the throat.

Contrasting with these, but still in the same family is the bluebird, of purest sky-blue above and tinged with chestnut below. This is probably the best loved of North American birds. In this it has a rival, the American robin, which looks very similar to a European blackbird except that it has a red breast.

Another sweet singer is the European robin. It sings the whole year round except for the month of August. About the size of a sparrow, it is brown with a red breast. A near cousin of the robin is the nightingale, another small brown bird that skulks among the bushes and is hard to see. It sings only during May but during that month it sings both day and night.

The songs that we associate with these birds are what scientists call *primary songs*. They are loud and are usually concerned with attracting a mate, defending territory and acting as warnings to other birds that danger is near. Many also have another type of song, the *secondary song* or *subsong*. These songs are as important as primary songs.

▼ When the first settlers reached America from England and saw a bird with a red breast they called it a robin. And like its European relative it, too, is sometimes called the robin redbreast. Here it is, the American robin, one of the best-known of the thrush family.

▼ Although the European robin is often called the robin redbreast, it would be more correct to say it has a red throat and face as well.

SUNBIRDS – THE SAME BUT DIFFERENT

Everybody has heard of hummingbirds. Few people have heard of sunbirds, apart from those who know tropical Africa well, although there are also some sunbirds in southern Asia and Australia. Yet hummingbirds and sunbirds both look very much alike and behave in a very similar manner, although they are not even closely related. This alone is an interesting scientific fact.

Both are small, both have a beautiful iridescent plumage; and both feed either on nectar or small insects, taken from bright flowers. But there are two important ways in which they differ from each other. The first is that hummingbirds sip nectar while hovering in front of a flower. They can do this because they have very long bills. Sunbirds also sip nectar, but they have to perch on the flower to do so, because their bills are much shorter.

There is another important difference. Both kinds of bird make very small nests in which the female lays two very small eggs. But the nest of a hummingbird is always a neat, delicate cup perched on a twig. A sunbird's nest is equally delicate but it is hung from a twig, forming a kind of bag with an entrance near the top. It is also untidy, looking ragged and with a tail of the nesting material hanging loosely from it.

▼ The yellow-breasted sunbird of south-east Asia clings to its ragged-looking nest. The nest is made of pieces of dried grass held together by cobwebs.

▲ A beautiful golden-winged sunbird perches with its wings partly open. Its curved bill is also visible.

▶ A male sunbird looks very like a hummingbird. It also has a very similar way of life. But the two live on opposite sides of the world, and are not related.

ORIOLES

There are two kinds of orioles. The two kinds look alike but belong to two different families. The true orioles, of the family Oriolidae, are found from Europe to Australia and across Asia and in Africa.

The best-known of the true orioles is the golden oriole. This is a striking yellow and black bird. Several other species of oriole are also the same colours.

The second kind of oriole belong to the family Icteridae, a quite different family. They are called the American orioles. The best-known of the American orioles is also a striking yellow and black. It is called the Baltimore oriole and it is best-known because it was first painted by John James Audubon, the great American naturalist.

◄ A golden oriole at its nest feeding its young. Their eyes are not yet open and their covering of down shows clearly.

John James Audubon

Audubon was born in Louisiana in 1780. He was sent to Paris where he studied drawing. On his return his father sent him to run a plantation but nothing could hold back his artistic talents. For 15 years Audubon spent all the time he could spare exploring the forests of America, painting animals, especially birds. And you cannot paint a thing well without learning a lot about it. Audubon's massive book, *Birds of America*, finished when he was 58, with its many exquisite pictures, formed a landmark in the study of natural history. It is one of the most valuable books on birds of all time.

◄ A fine example of the paintings of Audubon. It shows three Baltimore orioles, the two parents and a young one clinging to the nest.

SPARROWS AND WEAVERS

Once, the house sparrow was the most familiar of all birds in Europe, but that was in the days when transport was horse-drawn. With a short hard beak for cracking seeds, including grains, the sparrow fed in the fields of cereal crops and on the undigested grains in horse dung. With the coming of the motor car horses disappeared and sparrows became less numerous. But though its numbers may have fallen, it has now spread far beyond the continent of Europe, its original home. Reaching North America in the 1860s, it is now a firmly established resident there.

The house sparrow builds its nest in a tree or bush only if there is no building near. On houses it builds large untidy nests of straw. It may seem odd that it goes to the trouble of collecting so much straw but it belongs to the weaver family.

▲ The common European house sparrow has been taken to many other parts of the world by English-speaking settlers. Today it is found in North America, South Africa, Australia and New Zealand.

▲ A tree sparrow is very like the house sparrow but has a chestnut crown, not a grey one like the house sparrow. It always nests in trees, never on houses.

Weavers at work

Weavers, or weaverbirds as they are sometimes called, are among the most expert of nest-builders. They build beautifully-woven, hanging nests.

Weavers often nest in colonies. The most striking of these colonies belong to the sociable weaver. In the thorny branches of acacia trees on the African plains there are often huge masses of straw and grass 3m (10ft) high and 2m (6½ft) or more across. These are apartment houses made up of 30 or more nests all packed together and covered with a thatched roof. The sociable weavers responsible for these colonies work together to build them.

THE MOST NUMEROUS BIRD

▼ As the sun sinks in the west, all the starlings around gather in small groups. These join up into large flocks. They then make their way to their roosts. There they fly around in their thousands, sometimes even in their millions, before settling in the trees for the night. The common starling (**inset**) is a handsome bird and can be a useful one. But by sheer weight of numbers it has become a pest. Where it roosts in trees its droppings foul the leaves and often kill the trees.

As a group, the starlings have beautiful plumage as the names of some of them suggest, such as the glossy starlings and the superb starling. At first sight, the common starling is the most drab. It looks a very ordinary black bird, but if you look carefully at it in spring, when its new plumage catches the spring sunshine, its feathers shimmer like a rainbow.

Two hundred years ago the common starling was widely kept as a pet, largely because of its song and its ability to mimic sounds. Since then it has increased in numbers and spread across Europe to Iceland. It has also been taken around the world, to North America, South Africa, Australia and New Zealand.

The successful immigrant
Everywhere it has flourished and spread. From a few pairs released into a New York park it has spread across the United States to the Pacific and northwards into Canada. Wherever it goes it becomes noteworthy for its habit of roosting in large numbers, in reed-beds and trees and on buildings in cities. A single roost may contain a million or more birds, and before settling down for the night they may fly round, wheeling and circling in huge flocks.

Starlings are adept at mimicking sounds, including songs of other birds and the human voice. One account is about how, from an empty football ground, came the roar of spectators urging on the players. The only living thing there was a flock of starlings in a tree, who were mimicking the crowd.

BOWERBIRDS

In many species of birds the male and the female of a pair work together to build the nest. Sometimes it is the female that does most of the work. Sometimes it is the male, and in some species the male does nothing at all towards it. Bowerbirds have a way that is all their own. The female builds the nest in which to lay her eggs. The male also builds, but it is something entirely different. He builds a bower.

Bowerbirds live in Australia and the neighbouring island of New Guinea. As the breeding season begins, the male bowerbird chooses a clearing on the forest floor. He collects sticks and lays them out to make a platform. Then he collects more sticks and pushes them into the platform so that they stand upright in two rows.

After this he decorates this bower. He picks flowers, toadstools, and anything else that is bright and lays it in the bower. One bowerbird paints the bower with the juices of different berries. For this he uses a brush. He frays the end of a stick and dips this into the juice.

Then, when everything is ready, he attracts the female into the bower by showing off to her the few bright feathers he has in his plumage. The two play for a while in the bower, chasing each other up and down between the two rows of sticks. After that they mate and the hen goes away, to build a nest, lay her eggs and bring up her family, without his help.

▼ This is a fully-grown male satin bowerbird. He is starting to decorate the bower with flowers he has picked.

◄ A female satin bowerbird waiting in the bower of upright sticks built by the male. A young male, who has not yet grown the satin plumage, displays to her in his first attempt at courtship.

BIRDS-OF-PARADISE

▲ This red bird-of-paradise is a male. The female is less showy. The red plumes that give him his name are hidden until he is ready to court the female. Then he will spread them in all their beauty. A male of the Emperor of Germany's bird-of-paradise (**inset**) prepares to court the female. He will hop about the branches calling loudly and blowing out his silky green throat. This display of colour makes the female ready to breed.

Four hundred years ago, Ferdinand Magellan, the famous Portuguese explorer, visited new Guinea. He sent some bird skins back to the king of Spain. It is said that when the king saw them he said such beautiful birds must come from Paradise. The people of New Guinea called the birds *manukdewata*, meaning bird of the gods.

Fine feathers, fine birds

Birds-of-paradise, as they have since been known, are the most beautiful birds in the world, apart from the hummingbirds. But to see a male bird-of-paradise beside the female it is hard to believe they belong to the same species. The female is a drab brown while the male is covered with bright feathers. Moreover, he has bunches of even more splendid plumes, on his head or body, and usually has long tail plumes as well.

He uses this splendid plumage for courting the female bird-of-paradise. In addition to showing off his feathers to her he goes through elaborate dances, either on the ground or perched in the trees. At the same time he utters loud shrieks and whistles.

The hen seems to take no notice of this show but eventually she mates with him. Then she goes to the nest she has built and lays her eggs. She alone incubates the eggs and feeds and cares for the babies. The male does nothing to help. He merely amuses himself showing off, singing and dancing.

There are 41 different species of bird-of-paradise. They range in size from about 23cm (9in), the size of a small thrush, to about 40cm (16in), the size of a small crow, not including their long tails. The Princess Stephanie Bird-of-Paradise has tail feathers 61cm (24in) long although the rest of the body is barely 20çm (8in) in length. Birds-of-paradise are now protected, but their beautiful feathers were very popular at the beginning of this century for decorating women's hats.

THE CROW FAMILY

All sorts of birds are called crows, especially if they are fairly large, black, and have a strong bill and a harsh voice. There are, for example, the piping crow, the rain crow, and the bald crow. These, however, belong to totally different families. In fact, to the scientist they are not crows at all. When *ornithologists* speak of crows they are referring to members of the crow family. This includes true crows, as well as the rook, magpie and jay. Not all of these are black. Indeed, some jays have very bright plumage. The Steller jay, for instance, is a beautiful bright blue.

The crow family as a whole includes probably the most clever of all birds. One of them, the jackdaw, was once popular as a pet because of its clever ways. But it also has a reputation of stealing bright objects, such as jewellery. The magpie shares this reputation. There is even an opera, *The Thieving Magpie*, in which this habit of the magpie plays an important part.

Members of the crow family are unpopular with farmers because they steal fruit and other crops. They also have a bad name because they kill smaller birds and rob their nests. They also eat the flesh of dead birds and in this way act as scavengers.

True crows are good mimics. They rival parrots in the way they imitate sounds, words and the calls of other birds.

▼ We think of the crow family as black birds with little colour in their plumage. This Siberian jay is by contrast a splendid blue bird. Yet it belongs to the crow family.

▲ The common jay also has bright feathers. In autumn jays eat many acorns and bury others to eat later. A jay can find an acorn it has buried even when snow covers the ground.

◀ Rooks are European members of the crow family. They are black except for their grey bill and a bare, grey-white face patch at the base of the bill. Young rooks lack this face patch and so look a little like the all-black carrion crow. Members of the crow family are found throughout the world, apart from southern parts of South America, central Australia and New Zealand.

GLOSSARY

Aftershaft The small tuft of down on a bird's feather near the base of the vane (see page 6).

Archaeopteryx The lizard-like prehistoric animal from which today's birds are descended.

Arid Regions which are very dry because they have little rainfall or dew.

Bird-of-prey A bird that catches other living creatures for its food.

Breastbone The thin flat bone in the chest to which the ribs are joined.

Casque A horny helmet-like growth on the head of some birds, for example the cassowary.

Classify To arrange things scientifically in groups, in which everything in the group is related.

Clutch The eggs laid by a female bird each time she starts to rear a family.

Colony Group of birds of the same type living together.

Crop Part of the bird's digestive system where food is stored before it goes into the stomach.

Crustacean Animal such as a crab or lobster with a hard, crust-like shell.

Cryptic The patterning and colouring of an animal's coat or feathers so that it blends with its background and is difficult to see.

Gizzard The second part of a bird's stomach, where tough food is ground down.

Hibernate/hibernation Some animals survive the winter by going into a type of sleep. They become active again when the weather becomes warmer.

Incubation The period during which adult birds keep their eggs warm until their young are ready to leave the egg. Most birds incubate their eggs by sitting on them, but some, such as the penguins and brush turkeys, do not.

Keel The ridge or crest that runs along the breastbone of a bird.

Lagoon Shallow stretch of salt water almost separated from the sea by a low sandbank.

Mammal An animal that is fed on its mother's milk when it is a baby.

Mandibles The bony jaws which make up a bird's beak.

Migration A long journey made by some birds, usually twice a year and usually to avoid bad weather conditions in one of the areas where they live.

Nest-parasite A bird that lays its eggs in the nest of another bird and does nothing at all to help in rearing its young.

New World The continents of North and South America.

Old World The continents of Europe, Africa and Asia.

Ornithologist Someone who studies birds.

Oviparous An animal that lays eggs from which its young hatch.

Parasite A plant or animal that takes food and nourishment directly from another plant or animal. Bird parasites rob other birds of their food.

Plumage Another word for a birds' coat of feathers.

Primary song The main song of a bird, the one that we usually hear. It is usually concerned with defending territory and attracting a mate.

Quill The central shaft of a feather.

▼ A hen ostrich, her wing and tail feathers fluffed out over her eggs, dozes in the sun of southern Africa.

Reptile Cold-blooded animal, such as a crocodile or snake.

Roost The place where a bird perches to sleep, usually at night.

Scavenger Animal that eats the flesh of dead animals.

Secondary song A song, quieter than the primary song, that some birds have.

Species A group of animals or plants that look alike and behave in the same way, and are different from all others.

Squab The name for a young pigeon or dove.

Stoop The swift dive made by falcons to catch their prey.

Subsong Another term for secondary song.

Talon The strong claw of a bird-of-prey.

Temperate Those parts of the world where the temperature is not extreme, neither very hot nor very cold.

Thermal Rising current of warm air.

Tropics The areas of the world between the Tropic of Cancer in the north and the Tropic of Capricorn in the south, where the climate is usually hot.

Tundra The great areas of the northern hemisphere where only the surface of the ground ever thaws, the rest is permanently frozen.

Vane The flat part of a feather each side of the shaft.

Viviparous An animal that gives birth to live young.

Wattle Folds of bare skin on the heads of some birds, such as turkeys.

▲ Its striking black and white colouring and long tail give the magpie a very distinctive appearance. The magpie is a member of the crow family.

◄ A group of white storks resting among the tall grasses of a plain in southern Africa.

INDEX

Acknowledgments

Aquila, Ardea,
Australia House, A
Borgioli and G
Cappelli, A
Christiansen, Bruce
Coleman, S Frugis, L
Gaggero, I Holmasen,
Eric Hosking, Archivio
IGDA, Jacana, Frank
Lane, A Margiocco, J
Markham, NHPA, B
Petterson, S Prato, T
Suominen, Survival
Anglia, BE Swahn, Tio
J Johanisson, G
Tomsich.